HIGH SCHOOL CHECKLIST
FOR 9TH, 10TH, 11TH, 12TH GRADE STUDENTS

PREPARE
FOR
COLLEGE

CHECKLIST

SHAY SPIVEY, BSW, MSW

PREPARE FOR COLLEGE: HIGH SCHOOL CHECKLIST

PREPARE FOR COLLEGE

HIGH SCHOOL CHECKLIST

FOR 9TH, 10TH, 11TH, 12TH GRADE STUDENTS

BY

SHAY SPIVEY, BSW, MSW

TABLE OF CONTENTS

Brief Summary

About the Author

Introduction

Freshman Year Checklist

Sophomore Year Checklist

Junior Year Checklist

Senior Year Checklist

The Next Step is Up to You

Contact Shay Spivey

Other Books by Shay Spivey

BRIEF SUMMARY

Congratulations! You're a high school student!

Are you prepared for college?

Prepare for College: High School Checklist provides a checklist of important "things to do" during your freshman, sophomore, junior, and senior year of high school.

Quick and easy to read! ***Prepare for College: High School*** Checklist is for parents and students who want to know what to do each year to prepare for college.

ABOUT THE AUTHOR

Author and Social Worker, Shay Spivey, was awarded over $100,000 in college scholarships to fund her college education as an adult student and single parent. Shay earned her Bachelor and Master of Social Work from Indiana University.

With her help and guidance, students have accessed more than $1 million dollars in scholarships and free financial aid. The Scholarship Advisor Program founder has written several books that show students and families how to access free money for education.

In an effort to pay it forward, Shay teaches scholarship workshops in partnership with schools and organizations that make education more accessible for disadvantaged students.

DREAM. PREPARE. SUCCEED.

PREPARE FOR COLLEGE:

FRESHMAN YEAR CHECKLIST

Included in the Freshman Year Checklist

Brief Summary

Introduction

Other Books by Shay Spivey

Meet the School Counselor

Get Involved

Community Service

Academic Resume

College Visits

Have a Productive Summer

Scholarships and Financial Aid

Prepare for Sophomore Year

Summary

INTRODUCTION

Freshman year is an exciting and apprehensive period for first-time high school students and parents.

Have you and your family started preparing for college?

It's not uncommon for students and their parents to be nervous when it's time to prepare for college. The anxiety stems from not knowing exactly what to do or how to prepare for college. To add to the stress, most start their preparation very late. In order to reduce the stress you may feel at this time, it's important to be organized and well prepared. This book was written with you in mind, to help you prepare for college.

Here are several important tasks you should keep in mind during your freshman year.

MEET THE SCHOOL COUNSELORS

Most high schools have a variety of college resources available, but sometimes you have to ask. There are guidance counselors, college and career counselors, education centers, career service offices, clubs, and organizations. They furnish a list of scholarship opportunities to students that ask. So, ask your high school staff what college services are available.

Guidance Counselor

One of the many roles of a high school guidance counselor is to help students prepare for college. They are a FREE resource available to you so use them. Show up at their office, ask questions, and let them know that you're interested in going to college.

College Counselor

High school college counselors are the best-kept secrets around! They work directly with high school students alongside guidance counselors on campus. College counselors help high school students prepare for college by exploring each student's personal interests and guiding them through the application process. Another important service provided by high school college counselors is connecting students with resources such as scholarships and financial aid. Most students and their families are not aware that their high school provides this service. I encourage students to seek out and engage their high school college counselors.

Things to talk about:

-Create a four-year plan.

-What courses should I take to prepare for college?

-Does the school offer college planning events?

GET INVOLVED

Colleges are interested in students that are well-rounded. To compete, it's important to get involved in one or more activities outside of the classroom - and stay involved. If your academic qualifications are not excellent, colleges may dig deeper into your background to look at your civic engagement and extracurricular activities. This may be the edge you need to access the college of your dreams.

In addition to school extracurricular activities, students should also consider getting involved in the following activities and adding the experience to their academic resume.

-Summer Camps for Teens
-Career Exploration Programs
-Community service
-College Mentoring Programs

College Mentoring Program

I encourage you to get involved with a local college mentoring program in your area. College mentoring programs prepare middle and high school students for college success. They offer a variety of services including but not limited to guidance counseling and individualized instructional services. It's a great idea to participate in one of these programs because colleges often partner with local programs and sometimes provide scholarships to participants.

College mentoring programs work toward the goal of college access in a variety of ways. Some common community service program activities include:

Increasing academic readiness

College mentoring programs

College admissions counseling

Career counseling and shadowing

Assistance with financial aid forms

Course selection guidance

College application help

College campus visits

College entrance exam preparation

Study skills workshops

Parent workshops

Academic support

Motivational support

Tutoring

Service learning opportunities

COMMUNITY SERVICE

By participating in community service and volunteering, you can increase your chances of winning free money for college. Colleges seek promising students that will give back to their community and school during their college years and beyond. Volunteer experience sets your application apart from the other applications that scholarship organizations review.

Service Before College

Colleges sometimes offer scholarships to students that have a consistent history of community service. Community scholarships are available for students under 18, some for students as young as 10.

Service During College

Colleges also offer community service-based scholarships to students in exchange for a commitment to volunteer a certain number of hours while attending school. Be sure to ask your college about service-based scholarships.

The Best Kind of Community Service

Choose a volunteer opportunity that really matters to you - that is the best kind of community service. You will gain valuable experience and make a positive difference in the community. Let's face it; we are all busy. Finding time to volunteer can be a challenge and giving back through community service takes effort and commitment.

Where to Find Community Service and Volunteer Opportunities:

Animal rescue shelter

Aquarium or zoo

Environmental groups

Food pantries and soup kitchens

Fundraising walks and runs

Homeless Shelters

Hospitals

Libraries

Local nonprofit or charitable organizations

Museums

Nursing home or senior citizens centers

Parks

Political campaigns

Religious organization

Schools

Summer camps

Websites:

www.volunteermatch.org

www.idealist.org

www.createthegood.org

ACADEMIC RESUME

Keep track of your activities.

An academic resume is a brief summary of your personal and academic accomplishments. The goal is to provide a brief, organized view of your high school experience in a professional format.

If you do not have an academic resume, create one and continuously update it with new activities and experiences.

Academic Resume Outline

Academic Resume
Your name
Mailing address
Email address
Phone number(s)

High School Information
Name of high school
GPA

Academic Achievement
Honor roll
Special classes
Awards

Program Involvement
Extracurricular Activities
Special Programs
Workshops and camps
Clubs

Community Service
Volunteer experience

Internship or Employment Experience
Internships / Employment

COLLEGE VISIT

Exposure to the college environment is important. Visiting a college campus provides students with a preview of college life. Families will have the opportunity to ask questions and see the campus to determine if the school is a good fit. You can visit a college in person or via a virtual tour.

In Person

Walk the campus to get a good feel for the atmosphere. Your freshman year is a great time to contact the college admissions office and schedule an official tour. You can also schedule an overnight visit.

Virtual Tour

You can take a virtual campus tour online. Visit www.campustours.com or www.ecampustours.com

HAVE A PRODUCTIVE SUMMER

Make your Summer Count!

Try new things! Summers are a great time to participate in community service, summer camps for teens, career exploration programs, and summer classes. Spend this time wisely, don't waste it.

Pre-College Summer Programs

Have you considered taking college courses before you graduate high school? Are you curious about college life? Pre-college summer programs are a great way to make new friends, sample college life, and take college courses. To learn more, you can call or visit the college website of your choice.

Family Vacations

Going on a family vacation? Try to include a college campus visit while you're in another city. This is a terrific way to include your family in your planning for college.

SCHOLARSHIPS & FINANCIAL AID

Freshman year is not too early to think about how you will pay for college.

College can be quite expensive, so you have to think about how you will pay for it. Can your family afford to pay college tuition out of pocket? Or will you need financial assistance? How much money will you need? These are things you should consider before applying for college. If you need extra financial help, you can get these from scholarships, grants, and loans available to both students and their parents.

How Will You Pay for College?

Think about it. Talk about it. Make a plan.

Find College Scholarships

Do you want free money for college? Freshman year is a good time to search for scholarships and free financial aid on these free websites:

FastWeb.com

Scholarships.com

StudentAid.Ed.gov

CollegeBoard.org

FindTuition.com

Unigo.com

CollegeToolkit.com

Understanding
Scholarships and Financial Aid

Scholarships:

Scholarships are gift-aid and do <u>not</u> require repayment. Applicants must meet basic eligibility criteria to be considered.

Grants:

Grants are gift-aid and do <u>not</u> require repayment.

Student Loans:

Loans are available as a means of funding your education. Unlike gift aid, such as scholarships or grants, loans must be repaid. A subsidized student loan has no interest charged while the borrower is in school. An unsubsidized student loan charges interest at all periods, even while the borrower is enrolled in school.

Types of Scholarships

Merit-Based Scholarship:

Merit-based awards are based on a student's academic, artistic, athletic or other abilities.

Need-Based Scholarship:

Need-based awards are based on the student and family's financial record and require them to fill out a Free Application for Federal Student Aid (FAFSA) in order to qualify.

Student-Specific Scholarship:

Student-specific awards are given to applicants that identify with a specific group (gender, race, religion, family and medical history, etc.).

Career-Specific Scholarship:

Career-specific scholarships are awarded to students who plan to pursue a specific field of study. Often, the most generous awards are for students that pursue careers in high-need.

College-Specific Scholarship:

College-specific scholarships are offered by individual colleges to highly qualified applicants. These scholarships are awarded based on academic and personal achievement or personal circumstances.

PREPARE FOR COLLEGE

Sophomore year is an excellent time to start preparing for your future by exploring career options. To begin with, talk to people in career fields that you find exciting. You may also consider job shadowing opportunities and attend high school career fairs.

Think about:

What career is right for you?

What is interesting to you?

What is most important to you?

What career options fit your personality?

What are your unique strengths, skills, and talents?

SUMMARY

High School Freshman Year Checklist:

Meet the school counselor

Get involved

Community service

Create an academic resume

Go on college visits

Have a productive summer

Scholarships and financial aid

Prepare for your sophomore year

PREPARE FOR COLLEGE

SOPHOMORE YEAR CHECKLIST

Included in the Sophomore Year Checklist

Brief Summary

Introduction

Keep Your Grades Up

Meet the School Counselor

Take the PSAT

Career Exploration

Get Involved

Community Service Wins Scholarships

Academic Resume

Scholarships and Financial Aid

Have a Productive Summer

Prepare for Junior Year

Summary

INTRODUCTION

Sophomore year is an exciting year!

Have you and your family started preparing for college?

It's not uncommon for students and their parents to be nervous when it's time to prepare for college. The anxiety stems from not knowing exactly what to do or how to prepare for college. To add to the stress, most start their preparation very late. In order to reduce the stress you may feel at this time, it's important to be organized and well prepared. This book was written with you in mind, to help you prepare for college.

Here are several important tasks you should keep in mind during your sophomore year.

KEEP YOUR GRADES UP

The most important things that will determine whether you're qualified for college are your grades and test scores. To be more specific, colleges will check your grade point average (GPA), class rank, and college entrance exam scores. If you do well in these three areas, you're likely to gain admission into college.

However, if your grades and test scores have not been the best, there's still hope. Colleges also take other areas into consideration - some of which are listed in the following chapters.

It's also important to note that if you're interested in scholarships, you must keep a decent GPA during high school.

MEET THE SCHOOL COUNSELOR

Most high schools have a variety of college resources available, but sometimes you have to ask. There are guidance counselors, college and career counselors, education centers, career service offices, clubs, and organizations. These administrators often provide lists of scholarship opportunities to students that ask. So, ask your high school staff what college services are available.

Guidance Counselor

One of the many roles of a high school guidance counselor is to help students prepare for college. They are a FREE resource available to you, so use them. Visit their office, ask questions, and let them know that you're interested in going to college.

College Counselor

High school college counselors are the best-kept secrets around! They work directly with high school students alongside guidance counselors on campus. College counselors help high school students prepare for college by exploring each student's personal interests and guiding him or her through the application process. Another important service provided by high school college counselors is connecting students with resources such as scholarships and financial aid. Most students and their families are not aware that their high school provides this service. I encourage students to seek out and engage their high school college counselors.

Things to talk about:

-Are you on track to graduate?

-Ask to see your transcript.

-Ask about upcoming college and career fairs.

-Ask about career assessments.

TAKE THE PSAT

Take the Preliminary Scholastic Assessment Test (PSAT)

If possible, take the PSAT during your sophomore and junior year. This is a great opportunity to get a feel for the upcoming college entrance exams. Contact your school counselor and request to take this test in September of your sophomore year.

CAREER EXPLORATION

Sophomore year is an excellent time to start exploring career options. To begin with, talk to people in career fields that you find exciting. You may also consider job shadowing opportunities and attend high school career fairs.

Career Assessment Test

A career assessment test can help high school and college students gain insight into what type of careers fit the student's personality. Free assessments are available online. However, you can also contact your school counselor or a college mentoring program to request a career assessment and personal evaluation.

Find the Right Major

www.mymajors.com

www.myplan.com

www.collegemajors101.com

Career Camps

Many colleges offer career exploration programs and camps during the school year as well as in the summer.

Questions:

What Career is right for You?

What is interesting to you?

What is most important to you?

What career options fit your personality?

What are your unique strengths, skills, and talents?

GET INVOLVED

Colleges are interested in students that are well-rounded. To compete, it's important to get involved in one or more activities outside of the classroom - and stay involved. If your academic qualifications are not excellent, colleges may dig deeper into your background to look at your civic engagement and extracurricular activities.

In preparation for college, students should also consider getting involved in the following activities and adding the experience to their academic resume.

-Summer Camps for Teens
-Career Exploration Programs
-Community service

College Mentoring Program

I encourage you to get involved with a local college mentoring program in your area. College mentoring programs prepare middle and high school students for college success. They offer a variety of services including but not limited to guidance counseling and individualized instructional services. It's a great idea to participate in one of these programs because colleges often partner with local programs and sometimes provide scholarships to participants.

These programs work toward the goal of college access in a variety of ways. Some common program activities include:

Increasing academic readiness

College mentoring programs

College admissions counseling

Career counseling and shadowing

Assistance with financial aid forms

Course selection guidance

College application help

College campus visits

College entrance exam preparation

Study skills workshops

Parent workshops

Academic support

Motivational support

Tutoring

Service learning opportunities

COMMUNITY SERVICE WINS SCHOLARSHIPS

By participating in community service and volunteering, you can increase your chances of winning free money for college. Colleges seek promising students that will give back to their community and school during their college years and beyond. Volunteer experience sets your application apart from the other applications that scholarship organizations review.

Service before College

Colleges sometimes offer scholarships to students that have a consistent history of community service. Community scholarships are available for students under 18, some for students as young as 10.

Service during College

Colleges also offer community service-based scholarships to students in exchange for a commitment to volunteer a certain number of hours while attending school. Be sure to ask your college about service-based scholarships.

The Best Kind of Community Service

Choose a volunteer opportunity that really matters to you - that is the best kind of community service. You will gain valuable experience and make a positive difference in the community. Let's face it; we are all busy. Finding time to volunteer can be a challenge and giving back through community service takes effort and commitment.

Where to Find Community Service and Volunteer Opportunities:

Animal rescue shelter

Aquarium or zoo

Environmental groups

Food pantries and soup kitchens

Fundraising walks and runs

Homeless Shelters

Hospitals

Libraries

Local nonprofit or charitable organizations

Museums

Nursing home or senior citizens centers

Parks

Political campaigns

Religious organization

Schools

Summer camps

Websites:

www.volunteermatch.org

www.idealist.org

www.createthegood.org

ACADEMIC RESUME

An academic resume is a brief summary of your personal and academic accomplishments. The goal is to provide a brief, organized view of your high school experience in a professional format.

If you have not already completed this step, create an academic resume or update the one you have.

Academic Resume Outline

Academic Resume
Your name
Mailing address
Email address
Phone number(s)

High School Information
Name of high school
GPA

Academic Achievement
Honor roll
Special classes
Awards

Program Involvement
Extracurricular activities
Special programs
Workshops and camps
Clubs

Community Service
Volunteer experience

Internship or Employment Experience
Internships / Employment

SCHOLARSHIPS & FINANCIAL AID

College can be quite expensive, so you have to think about how you will pay for it. Can your family afford to pay college tuition out of pocket? Or, will you need financial assistance? How much money will you need? These are things you should consider before applying for college. If you need extra financial help, you can get these from scholarships, grants, and loans available to both students and their parents.

How Will You Pay for College?

Think about it. Talk about it. Make a plan.

Find College Scholarships

Do you want free money for college? Junior year is a good time to search for scholarships and free financial aid on these free websites:

FastWeb.com

Scholarships.com

StudentAid.Ed.gov

CollegeBoard.org

FindTuition.com

Unigo.com

CollegeToolkit.com

Understanding
Scholarships and Financial Aid

Scholarships:

Scholarships are financial aid and do <u>not</u> require repayment. Applicants must meet basic eligibility criteria to be considered.

Grants:

Grants are financial aid and do <u>not</u> require repayment.

Student Loans:

Loans are available as a means of funding your education. Unlike gift aid, such as scholarships or grants, loans must be repaid. A *subsidized student loan* has no interest charged while the borrower is in school. An *unsubsidized student loan* charges interest at all periods, even while the borrower is enrolled in school.

Types of Scholarships

Merit-Based Scholarship:

Merit-based awards are based on a student's academic, artistic, athletic or other abilities.

Need-Based Scholarship:

Need-based awards are based on the student and family's financial record and require them to fill out a Free Application for Federal Student Aid (FAFSA) in order to qualify.

Student-Specific Scholarship:

Student-specific awards are given to applicants that identify with a specific group (gender, race, religion, family and medical history, etc.).

Career-Specific Scholarship:

Career-specific scholarships are awarded to students who plan to pursue a specific field of study. The most generous awards are for students that pursue careers in high-need.

College-Specific Scholarship:

College-specific scholarships are offered by individual colleges to highly qualified applicants. These scholarships are awarded based on academic and personal achievement, or personal circumstances.

HAVE A PRODUCTIVE SUMMER

Make your Summer Count!

Summers are a great time to participate in community service, summer camps for teens, career exploration programs, and summer classes. Spend this time wisely, don't waste it.

Volunteer in the US
Americorps.org
cityyear.org

Go Abroad! Go International!
Studying abroad can be an enriching experience. Check out these programs for high school students.
Iiepassport.org
Planetedu.com
Americorps.org
vfp.org
Youthinternational.org
Istc.org
Studyabroad.com

Counciltravel.com

unv.org

Pre-College Summer Programs

Have you considered taking college courses before you graduate high school? Are you curious about college life? Pre-college summer programs are a great way to make new friends, sample college life, and take college courses. To learn more, you can call or visit the college website of your choice.

Family Vacations

Going on a family vacation? Try to include a college campus visit while you're in another city. This is a terrific way to include your family in your planning for college.

PREPARE FOR JUNIOR YEAR

Your junior year is the most important year of your high school career. There's a lot to be done during your junior year so what can you do to prepare in advance?

Research Colleges

It's important for students and parents to research colleges so that students can get an idea of what colleges will be a good fit. Consider asking yourself the following questions:

What type of college is right for you?

4-year or 2-year

In-state or out-of-state

What colleges have my major?

What size campus would I like?

Housing options

Tuition cost

Helpful websites:

www.unigo.com

nces.ed.gov/collegenavigator

www.chegg.com

www.cappex.com

SUMMARY

High School Sophomore Year Checklist:

Keep your grades up

Meet with the school counselor

Take the PSAT

Explore careers

Get involved

Community service wins scholarships

Create an academic resume

Learn about scholarships and financial aid

Have a productive summer

Prepare for your junior year

PREPARE FOR COLLEGE:
JUNIOR YEAR CHECKLIST

Included in the Junior Year Checklist

Brief Summary

Introduction

Keep Your Grades Up

Meet the School Counselor

Take the PSAT

Take College Entrance Exams

Research Colleges

Request Information from Colleges

Campus Visits

Attend College Fairs

Career Exploration

Get Involved

Have a Productive Summer

Academic Resume

Scholarships and Financial Aid

Community Service Wins Scholarships

Prepare for Senior Year

Summary

INTRODUCTION

Congratulations! You're a high school junior!

Are you prepared for college? If you plan to attend college after graduation, junior year is a great time to start preparing.

It's not uncommon for students and their parents to be nervous when it's time to prepare for college. The anxiety stems from not knowing exactly what to do or how to prepare for college. To add to the stress, most start their preparation very late. In order to reduce the stress you may feel at this time, it's important to be organized and well prepared. This book was written with you in mind, to help you prepare for college.

Here are several important tasks you should keep in mind during your junior year.

KEEP YOUR GRADES UP

The most important things that will determine whether you're qualified for college are your grades and test scores. To be more specific, colleges will check your grade point average (GPA), class rank, and college entrance exam scores. If you do well in these three areas, you're likely to gain admission into college. However, if your grades and test scores have not been the best, there's still hope. Colleges also take other areas into consideration - some of which are listed in the following chapters.

Junior year grades are the most important. When you apply to colleges during your senior year, the junior year report cards are the first grades they see.

It's important to note that if you're interested in scholarships, you must keep a decent GPA.

MEET THE SCHOOL COUNSELOR

Most high schools have a variety of college resources available, but sometimes you have to ask. There are guidance counselors, college and career counselors, education centers, career service offices, clubs, and organizations. They furnish a list of scholarship opportunities to students that ask. So, ask your high school staff what college services are available.

Guidance Counselor

One of the many roles of a high school guidance counselor is to help students prepare for college. They are a FREE resource available to you so use them. Show up at their office, ask questions, and let them know that you're interested in going to college.

College Counselor

High school college counselors are the best-kept secrets around! They work directly with high school students alongside guidance counselors on campus. College counselors help high school students prepare for college by exploring each student's personal interests and guiding them through the application process. Another important service provided by high school college counselors is connecting students with resources such as scholarships and financial aid. Most students and their families are not aware that their high school provides this service. I encourage students to seek out and engage their high school college counselors.

Things to talk about:

-Are you on track to graduate?

-Ask to see your transcript.

-Ask about college options.

-Ask about scholarship opportunities.

-Your school counselor is also a great source for letters of recommendation.

TAKE THE PSAT

Preliminary Scholastic Assessment Test (PSAT)

Take the PSAT during your junior year to qualify for the National Merit Scholarship. Contact your school counselor about taking this test in September of your junior year.

Once you take the PSAT colleges will start sending you information!

TAKE COLLEGE ENTRANCE EXAMS

This is the year that students take a college entrance exam - a key college admissions requirement. The two most common exams are the SAT and ACT. Juniors should take each test at least once during the school year. Students can take each test as many times as they like, but there's a cost for each exam.

American College Testing (ACT)
Website: www.act.org

Scholastic Assessment Test (SAT)
Website: www.collegeboard.org

Fee Waiver
Did you know about college entrance exam fee waivers for income-eligible students? Request a waiver. Fee waivers are available for families that qualify. School counselors are given a limited number of waivers so request in advance. For more information, contact your school counselor.

Registration

You must register in advance for each college entrance exam, sometime months in advance. So register early.

Test Prep

There are many test prep classes, books, and websites. Some are free, and others charge a fee. The school counselor and local library are good places to start your search for free options.

RESEARCH COLLEGE

The junior year is especially important for students and parents to research colleges because students will start submitting college admission applications in the fall semester of their senior year. To prepare, students and parents should start asking themselves important questions like:

What type of college is right for you?

2-year or 4-year

In-state or out-of-state

What colleges have your major?

What size campus would you like?

Housing options

Tuition cost

Websites:

www.unigo.com

nces.ed.gov/collegenavigator

www.chegg.com

www.cappex.com

REQUEST INFORMATION FROM COLLEGES

If you're interested in learning more about a college, request information from their admissions office by calling or filling out a request form on the college website.

Do you want colleges to reach out to you? All you have to do is give them your address.

College Search Sites

www.allaboutcollege.com

www.collegeboard.org

www.usnews.com/education

www.petersons.com

www.collegeview.com

www.collegeconfidential.com

CAMPUS VISITS

Exposure to the college environment is important. Visiting a college campus provides students with a preview of college life. Families will have the opportunity to ask questions and see the campus to determine if the school is a good fit. You can visit a college in person or via virtual tour.

In Person

Walk the campus to get a good feel for the atmosphere. Your junior year is a great time to contact the college admissions office and schedule an official tour. You can also schedule an overnight visit.

Virtual Tour

You can take a virtual campus tour online. Visit www.campustours.com or www.ecampustours.com

What will you do on a campus tour?

Meet an admissions representative

Take a tour

Walk the campus

Eat at the cafeteria

Look at dorm rooms

See classrooms

ATTEND COLLEGE FAIRS

College fairs are a one-stop shop to gather information from hundreds of colleges.

High schools, colleges, and other organizations host college fairs every year. College fairs give students a chance to learn about colleges and what they have to offer.

Will your high school be hosting a college fair? Check with your school counselor.

What to do at a College Fair:

Walk around

Ask questions

Look interested

Questions to ask:

Do they carry your major?

Are there special admissions requirements?

How much are tuition, room, and board?

What is the campus like?

Is on-campus housing available?

CAREER EXPLORATION

Prepare for the future by exploring career options. To begin with, talk to people in career fields that you find exciting. You may also consider job shadowing opportunities and attend high school career fairs.

Career Assessment Test

A career assessment test can help high school and college students gain insight into what type of careers fit the student's personality. Free assessments are available online. However, you can also contact your school counselor or a college mentoring program to request a career assessment and personal evaluation.

Find the Right Major

www.mymajors.com

www.myplan.com

www.collegemajors101.com

Career Camps

Many colleges offer career exploration programs and camps during the school year as well as in the summer.

What Career is Right for You?

What is interesting to you?

What is most important to you?

What career options fit your personality?

What are your unique strengths, skills, and talents?

GET INVOLVED

Colleges are interested in students that are well-rounded. To compete, it's important to get involved in one or more activities outside of the classroom - and stay involved. If your academic qualifications are not excellent, colleges may dig deeper into your background to look at your civic engagement and extracurricular activities. This may be the edge you need to access the college of your dreams.

In preparation for college, students should also consider getting involved in the following activities and adding the experience to their academic resume.

-Summer Camps for Teens
-Career Exploration Programs
-Community service

College Mentoring Program

I encourage you to get involved with a local college mentoring program in your area. College mentoring programs prepare middle and high school students for college success. They offer a variety of services including but not limited to guidance counseling and individualized instructional services. It's a great idea to participate in one of these programs because colleges often partner with local programs and sometimes provide scholarships to participants.

These programs work toward the goal of college access in a variety of ways. Some common program activities include:

Increasing academic readiness

College mentoring programs

College admissions counseling

Career counseling and shadowing

Assistance with financial aid forms

Course selection guidance

College application help

College campus visits

College entrance exam preparation

Study skills workshops

Parent workshops

Academic support

Motivational support

Tutoring

Service learning opportunities

HAVE A PRODUCTIVE SUMMER

Make your Summer Count!

Summers are a great time to participate in community service, summer camps for teens, career exploration programs, and summer classes. Spend this time wisely, don't waste it.

Volunteer in the US

Americorps.org

cityyear.org

Go Abroad! Go International!

Studying abroad can be an enriching experience. Check out these programs for high school students.

Iiepassport.org

Planetedu.com

Americorps.org

vfp.org

Youthinternational.org

Istc.org

Studyabroad.com

Counciltravel.com

unv.org

Pre-College Summer Programs

Have you considered taking college courses before you graduate high school? Are you curious about college life? Pre-college summer programs are a great way to make new friends, sample college life, and take college courses. To learn more, you can call or visit the college website of your choice.

Family Vacations

Going on a family vacation? Try to include a college campus visit while you're in another city. This is a terrific way to include your family in your planning for college.

ACADEMIC RESUME

An academic resume is an organized view of your high school experience in a professional format.

If you have not already, create an academic resume or update the one you have.

Academic Resume Outline

Academic Resume
Your name
Mailing address
Email address
Phone number(s)

High School Information
Name of high school
GPA

Academic Achievement
Honor roll
Special classes
Awards

Program Involvement
Extracurricular Activities
Special Programs
Activities
Workshops and camps
Clubs

Community Service
Volunteer experience

Internship or Employment Experience
Internships / Employment

SCHOLARSHIPS & FINANCIAL AID

College can be quite expensive, so you have to think about how you will pay for it. Can your family afford to pay college tuition out of pocket? Or will you need financial assistance? How much money will you need? These are things you should consider before applying for college. If you need extra financial help, you can get these from scholarships, grants, and loans available to both students and their parents.

How Will You Pay for College?

Think about it. Talk about it. Make a plan.

Find College Scholarships

Do you want free money for college? Junior year is a good time to search for scholarships and free financial aid on these free websites:

-FastWeb.com

-Scholarships.com

-StudentAid.Ed.gov

-CollegeBoard.org

-FindTuition.com

-Unigo.com

-CollegeToolkit.com

Understanding Scholarships and Financial Aid

Scholarships:

Scholarships are gift-aid and do <u>not</u> require repayment. Applicants must meet basic eligibility criteria to be considered.

Grants:

Grants are gift-aid and do <u>not</u> require repayment.

Student loans:

Loans are available as a means of funding your education. Unlike gift aid, such as scholarships or grants, loans must be repaid. A subsidized student loan has no interest charged while the borrower is in school. An unsubsidized student loan charges interest at all periods, even while the borrower is enrolled in school.

Types of Scholarships

Merit-based scholarships:

Merit-based awards are based on a student's academic, artistic, athletic or other abilities.

Need-based scholarships:

Need-based awards are based on the student and family's financial record and require them to fill out a Free Application for Federal Student Aid (FAFSA) in order to qualify.

Student-specific scholarships:

Student-specific awards are given to applicants that identify with a specific group (gender, race, religion, family and medical history, etc.).

Career-specific scholarship:

Career-specific scholarships are awarded to students who plan to pursue a specific field of study. Often, the most generous awards are for students that pursue careers in high-need.

College-specific scholarship:

College-specific scholarships are offered by individual colleges to highly qualified applicants. These scholarships are awarded based on academic and personal achievement or personal circumstances.

COMMUNITY SERVICE WINS SCHOLARSHIPS

By participating in community service and volunteering, you can increase your chances of winning free money for college. Colleges seek promising students that will give back to their community and school during their college years and beyond. Volunteer experience sets your application apart from the other applications that scholarship organizations review.

Service Before College

Colleges sometimes offer scholarships to students that have a consistent history of community service. Community scholarships are available for students under 18, some for students as young as 10.

Service During College

Colleges also offer community service-based scholarships to students in exchange for a commitment to volunteer a certain number of hours while attending school. Be sure to ask your college about service-based scholarships.

The Best Kind of Community Service

Choose a volunteer opportunity that really matters to you - that is the best kind of community service. You will gain valuable experience and make a positive difference in the community. Let's face it; we are all busy. Finding time to volunteer can be a challenge and giving back through community service takes effort and commitment.

Where to Find Community Service and Volunteer Opportunities:

Animal rescue shelter

Aquarium or zoo

Environmental groups

Food pantries and soup kitchens

Fundraising walks and runs

Homeless Shelters

Hospitals

Libraries

Local nonprofit or charitable organizations

Museums

Nursing home or senior citizens centers

Parks

Political campaigns

Religious organization

Schools

Summer camps

Websites:

www.volunteermatch.org

www.idealist.org

www.createthegood.org

PREPARE FOR COLLEGE

Your senior year will fly by. There's a lot to be done during your senior year so what can you do to prepare in advance?

Essays

Start working on your essay for college admissions and scholarship applications. If you need help writing a winning essay, check out any of the following suggestions:

Helpful website:

www.myessay.com

Helpful Book:

-How to Submit a Winning Scholarship Application: Secret Techniques I Used to Win $100,000 in College Scholarships by Shay Spivey

-Your local library is an excellent FREE resource.

List of Colleges

Do you know what colleges you plan to apply to next year? Be prepared to finalize your list of colleges by September of your senior year.

SUMMARY

High School Junior Year Checklist:

Keep Your Grades Up

Meet the School Counselor

Take PSAT

Take College Entrance Exams

Research Colleges

Request Information from Colleges

Campus Visits

Attend College Fairs

Career Exploration

Get Involved

Have a Productive Summer

Academic Resume

Scholarships and Financial Aid

Community Service Wins Scholarships

College Mentoring Programs

Prepare for Senior Year

PREPARE FOR COLLEGE
SENIOR YEAR CHECKLIST

Included in the Senior Year Checklist

Brief Summary

Introduction

Finish Strong

Meet the School Counselor

Request Letters of Recommendation

Request Transcript

Finish Essays

Get Organized

Apply to College

Take College Entrance Exams

Academic Resume

Scholarship Application Time

File a FAFSA

Choose a College

Deposits and Deadlines

Say Thank You

Summary

INTRODUCTION

Congratulations!

You finally made it - Senior Year.

There are many important events to plan for this year like prom, graduation ceremony, and college!

If you have been reading my books, you're on track and prepared for this final leg of the journey to college.

FINISH STRONG

Keep Your Grades Up.

Though junior grades are a college's first glimpse at you as a student, your senior grade point average (GPA) has the final say. Colleges require your final transcript and reserve the right to rescind their admissions invitation if your grades suddenly drop.

The most important things that will determine whether you're qualified for college are your grades and test scores. To be more specific, colleges will check your GPA, class rank, and college entrance exam scores. If you do well in these three areas, you're likely to gain admission into college. However, if your grades and test scores have not been the best, there's still hope. Colleges also take other areas into consideration - some of which are listed in following chapters.

When you apply to colleges during your senior year, the junior year report cards are the first grades they see. However, senior year grades are also very important. If you're interested in scholarships, you must keep a decent GPA.

MEET THE SCHOOL COUNSELOR

Senior Year: September

Are you on track to graduate?

Most high schools have a variety of college resources available, but sometimes you have to ask. There are guidance counselors, college and career counselors, education centers, career service offices, clubs, and organizations. Most high schools furnish a list of scholarship opportunities to students that ask. So, ask your high school staff what college services are available.

Guidance Counselor

One of the many roles of a high school guidance counselor is to help students prepare for college. They are a FREE resource available to you, so use them. Visit their office, ask questions, and let them know that you're interested in going to college.

College Counselor

High school college counselors are the best-kept secrets around! They work directly with high school students alongside guidance counselors on campus. College counselors help high school students prepare for college by exploring each student's personal interests and guiding him or her through the application process.

Another important service provided by high school college counselors is connecting students with resources such as scholarships and financial aid. Most students and their families are not aware that their high school provides this service. I encourage students to seek out and engage their high school college counselors.

Things to talk about:

-Are you on track to graduate?

-Request copies of your transcript.

-Request letters of recommendation.

-Ask about scholarship opportunities.

REQUEST LETTERS OF RECOMMENDATION

Senior Year: October

A letter of recommendation is written by a person who can describe your character, skills, and accomplishments. Students will need at least three letters of recommendation to include with college and scholarship applications. Colleges look closely at these letters and consider them a valuable external perspective about you as a person, peer, employee, student, and/or volunteer.

Who to Ask

You should request letters of recommendation from people who will write about you in a positive way and emphasize your strengths. Consider asking any of the following:

Teachers and professors
Counselors (school counselor or guidance counselor)
Employers, managers, supervisors, and coworkers

137

Religious leaders

Community service and volunteer activity leaders

Organization members and leaders

Coaches

REQUEST TRANSCRIPT

Senior Year: September

A transcript is an official record that shows a student's grades and a list of the courses taken. Most colleges and scholarship organizations request a copy of your high school transcripts as a part of the application package.

I encourage students to ask for 5-10 sealed copies well in advance of the college application season. To save time and money open one and make several copies to include as part of your application packages.

FINISH ESSAY

Senior Year: October/November

Students will need to write essays for college admissions and scholarship applications. The personal statement, or essay, is an important part of the application process. I encourage applicants to start early because writing is a process. The writing process will help applicants think about, and answer, questions like:

Why is college important to me?

Where am I coming from?

Where do I want to go?

What are my goals?

GET ORGANIZED

Senior Year: Summer before senior year

Many students and parents feel overwhelmed when they think about applying for college. Organization is the key to managing the college application process with ease. Staying organized and keeping all your information in one location makes it easier to prioritize, meet deadlines, and take advantage of valuable opportunities.

Create a College Binder

I encourage you to invest in a three-ring binder, or accordion file, to help stay organized. A college binder allows you to keep all your important application documents in one easy-to-access location.

Seniors should prepare in advance by having copies of the following documents on hand:

Transcript

Letters of recommendation

Admission letters

FAFSA submission confirmation page

College entrance exam scores

Community service write-up

Academic resume

Personal statement

Technology

Use your technical devices to stay on track. Cell phone alarms, tasks, and calendars are excellent tools that you can use to program important dates and helpful reminders.

APPLY TO COLLEGE

Senior Year: October, November, December, January

Do you know what colleges you plan to apply to? Finalize your list of colleges by September of your senior year, as the application process will begin in the next few months. In addition, make sure to check application deadlines and write them on your calendar.

Apply

I highly encourage students to apply to multiple colleges. You want to have options. When submitting college admissions applications, students should prepare in advance follow the instructions and pay attention to the deadline.

Follow Instructions

It's important to note that colleges receive thousands of applications each year. They are looking for applicants that meet their eligibility criteria, follow instructions and submit their complete admissions application packages in a timely manner.

Each application will provide unique and specific instructions. When scholarship applicants do not follow instructions, they risk having their applications discarded.

Deadlines

Pay close attention to the application deadlines. Late applications may still be accepted, but possibly waitlisted.

Fee Waivers

Did you know about college application fee waivers for income-eligible students? Request a waiver, if applicable. Fee waivers are available for families that qualify. School counselors are given a limited number of waivers, so request in advance. For more information, contact your school counselor.

TAKE COLLEGE ENTRANCE EXAMS

Senior Year: October (Register); December/January (Test)

Students have the opportunity to take the college entrance exams, a key college admissions requirement, one last time. The two most common exams are the SAT and ACT. Juniors should take each test at least once during the school year. Students can take each test as many times as they like, but there's a cost for each exam.

American College Testing (ACT)
Website: www.act.org

Scholastic Assessment Test (SAT)
Website: www.collegeboard.org

Fee Waiver
Do you know about college entrance exam fee waivers for income-eligible students? Request a waiver, if applicable. Fee waivers are available for families that

qualify. School counselors are given a limited number of waivers, so request in advance. For more information, contact your school counselor.

Registration

You must register in advance for each college entrance exam. Some exams require registration months in advance, so register early.

Test Prep

There are many test prep classes, books, and websites. Some are free, and others charge a fee. The school counselor and local library are good places to start your search for free options.

ACADEMIC RESUME

Senior Year: September/October

At the beginning of your senior year, update your academic resume and send an updated copy with each college and scholarship application.

An academic resume is an organized view of your high school experience in a professional format.

If you have not already completed this step, create an academic resume or update the one you have.

Academic Resume Outline

Academic Resume
Your name
Mailing address
Email address
Phone number

High School Information
Name of high school
GPA

Academic Achievement
Honor roll
Special classes
Awards

Program Involvement
Extracurricular activities
Special programs
Workshops and camps
Clubs

Community Service
Volunteer experience

Internship or Employment Experience
Internships / Employment

SCHOLARSHIP APPLICATION TIME

Senior Year: October (start gathering documents); Senior Year: January, February, March, April, and May (application deadlines)

How Will You Pay for College?

Think about it. Talk about it. Make a plan.

College can be quite expensive, so you have to think about how you will pay for it. Can your family afford to pay college tuition out of pocket? Or, will you need financial assistance? How much money will you need? These are things you should consider before applying for college. If you need extra financial help, you can get these from scholarships, grants, and loans available to both students and their parents.

Find College Scholarships

Do you want free money for college? Junior year is a good time to search for scholarships and free financial aid on these free websites:

FastWeb.com

Scholarships.com

StudentAid.Ed.gov

CollegeBoard.org

FindTuition.com

Unigo.com

CollegeToolkit.com

Deadlines

Pay attention to the scholarship application deadlines. You have been preparing for this moment; do not miss important deadlines by relying on your memory. Write it down! The majority of scholarship applications are due between January and May (before fall admission).

FILE A FAFSA

Senior Year: March Deadline

FAFSA: Free Application for Federal Student Aid
Application method: Online
Website:www.fafsa.ed.gov
Cost: Free

Billions of dollars in federal financial aid are awarded each year. Eligibility is determined using the FAFSA. Federal financial aid can be accessed through the online application: Free Application for Federal Student Aid.

Did you complete the FAFSA? Some scholarships will ask for proof of your FAFSA application submission. I encourage parents to submit their tax information as soon as possible.

Financial Aid Award Letter

Seniors who have been accepted to a college will receive a financial aid award letter from that college around April. For families that cannot afford to pay for college out of pocket, this is the most important letter you will receive. This letter will break down the cost of college for your family.

Examine the financial aid award letter for the following types of financial aid:

-Free money (scholarships and grants)

-Loans

-Out of pocket costs

Understanding
Scholarships and Financial Aid

Scholarships:

Scholarships are gift-aid and do <u>not</u> require repayment. Applicants must meet basic eligibility criteria to be considered.

Grants:

Grants are gift-aid and do <u>not</u> require repayment.

Student Loans:

Loans are available as a means of funding your education. Unlike gift-aid, such as scholarships or grants, loans must be repaid. A subsidized student loan has no interest charged while the borrower is in school. An unsubsidized student loan charges interest at all periods, even while the borrower is enrolled in school.

Types of Scholarships

Merit-Based Scholarships:

Merit-based awards are based on a student's academic, artistic, athletic or other abilities.

Need-Based Scholarships:

Need-based awards are based on the student and family's financial record.

Student-Specific Scholarships:

Student-specific awards are given to applicants that identify with a specific group (gender, race, religion, family and medical history, etc.).

Career-Specific Scholarships:

Career-specific scholarships are awarded to students who plan to pursue a specific field of study. The most generous awards are often for students that pursue careers in high-need.

College-Specific Scholarships:

College-specific scholarships are offered by individual colleges to highly qualified applicants. These scholarships are awarded based on academic and personal achievement, or personal circumstances.

CHOOSE A COLLEGE

Senior Year: April

After you...

(1) Apply to several colleges,

(2) Receive admission decisions, and

(3) Receive your financial aid award letters,

I encourage you to compare all the offers before choosing a college. An unexpected offer might surprise you!

Officially Accept

Once you decide which college fits the majority of your needs and is affordable for your family, officially accept their admissions offer. Be sure to accept the financial aid package and make the required deposits. Most colleges have a May 1st acceptance deadline.

Be sure to send a courteous decline letter to the other colleges so that another student can have a chance to attend.

Decide on a college!

DEPOSITS AND DEADLINES

Senior Year: May 1st deadline

Once you have chosen a college, determine if commuting or living on campus is right for you. If you decide to live on campus, determine the necessary next steps to inform the school. If you're ready to accept an admissions offer, find out what the college needs from you to make it official.

You do not want to lose out on opportunities because you missed the deadline.

Questions to ask:

Do you need to send a deposit? What is the deadline?

Have you notified the admissions department of your acceptance?

Have you politely declined other admission offers?

Have you completed your housing and meal plan requirements?

Have you scheduled and taken the advanced placement exams?

Did you send your final transcripts to the college of your choice?

SAY THANK YOU

Give yourself one more advantage by sending a thank you note. Not only is it good manners, but saying "thank you" shows your appreciation. I encourage you to send a thank you note to the people that wrote a letter of recommendation for you, and to every scholarship organization that gave you free money for college.

SUMMARY

High School Senior Year Checklist:

-Finish strong

-Meet the school counselor

-Request letters of recommendation

-Request transcript

-Finish essays

-Get organized

-Apply to college

-Take college entrance exams

-Create or update your academic resume

-Complete scholarship applications

-File a FAFSA

-Choose a college

-Be aware of deposits and deadlines

-Say "thank you."

THE NEXT STEP IS UP TO YOU

Good luck to you and your family as you prepare for college. I hope this information gets you one step closer to achieving your educational goals.

Knowledge is power!

Now that you know what to do your freshman, sophomore, junior, and senior year to prepare for college, what will you do with the information?

CONTACT

Thank you for reading!

I would love to receive your feedback after you finish reading. Please share your thoughts about this book by leaving a review wherever you made your purchase.

Email:

shayspivey@yahoo.com

Scholarship Blog:

www.scholarshipadvisor.blogspot.com

Author Blog:

www.shayspivey.blogspot.com

Facebook:

www.facebook.com/authorshayspivey

Twitter & Instagram:

@ShayMSpivey

OTHER BOOKS BY SHAY SPIVEY

Educate Girls Around the World: Good People Doing Good Work

FREE Money for Education Series:
How to Submit a Winning Scholarship Application: Secret Techniques I Used to Win $100,000 in College Scholarships

How to Find Scholarships and Free Financial Aid for Private High Schools

Where to Find FREE Money for College

FREE Tuition Colleges 2016

Find FREE Money for Graduate School

FREE Tuition Colleges for Adults 50+

Understanding Scholarships and Financial Aid

Comprensión De Becas Y Ayuda Financiera

Prepare for College Series:
Prepare for College Series: The Complete Collection
Prepare for College: Middle School Checklist
Prepare for College: Freshman Year Checklist
Prepare for College: Sophomore Year Checklist

Prepare for College: Junior Year Checklist
Prepare for College: Senior Year Checklist

Quick Reference Series:
FREE Online College Courses for Everyone
FREE Online Art Courses
FREE Online Biology Courses
FREE Online Business Courses
FREE Online Computer Courses
FREE Online Economics Courses
FREE Online Engineering Courses
FREE Online History Courses
FREE Online Law Courses
FREE Online Math Courses
FREE Online Philosophy Courses
FREE Online Psychology Courses
FREE Online State Programs

Made in United States
North Haven, CT
21 December 2021

13510717R00095